Alfred's Basic Piano Library

Prep Course

FOR THE YOUNG BEGINNER

Activity & Ear Training Book • Level D

Gayle Kowalchyk • E. L. Lancaster

A delightful workbook filled with a variety of fun activities,
the material reinforces musical concepts and includes well-planned listening activities
that develop ear-training skills.

Illustrations by Christine Finn   Art Direction by Ted Engelbart   Layout by Linda Lusk

Instructions for Use

1. This ACTIVITY & EAR TRAINING book is designed to be used with Alfred's PREP COURSE for the young beginner, LESSON BOOK D.

2. This book is coordinated page-by-page with the LESSON BOOK, and assignments are ideally made according to the instructions in the upper right corner of each page of the ACTIVITY & EAR TRAINING BOOK.

3. Many students enjoy completing these pages so much that they will want to go beyond the assigned material. However, it is best to wait until the indicated pages in the LESSON BOOK have been covered before the corresponding material in this book is studied.

4. This ACTIVITY & EAR TRAINING BOOK reinforces each concept presented in the LESSON BOOK and specifically focuses on the training and development of the ear. Rhythmic, melodic and harmonic concepts are drilled throughout the book to provide the necessary systematic reinforcement for the student.

5. Listening examples on certain pages (3–5, 7–12, 14, 16–18, 20–27, 29–42) are best completed at the lesson. Examples for these pages are given for the teacher (pages 43–48). All other pages may be assigned for home study, if so desired.

Use with Alfred's Basic Piano Library
PREP COURSE, Lesson D, pages 4–5.

Review

1. Your teacher will clap a rhythm pattern. Circle the pattern that you hear.

2. Your teacher will play a melody in the G POSITION.

   Draw the missing two eighth notes ( ) in the box.

3. Your teacher will play intervals of a 3rd or 5th. Circle the interval that you hear.

4. Your teacher will play a group of HARMONIC intervals. Circle the interval that you hear.

5. Your teacher will play a MODERATELY LOUD (*mf*) or SOFT (*p*) melody.
   Circle the answer that you hear.

6. Your teacher will play a melody.
   • Add a CRESCENDO sign ( ) UNDER the staff if the melody gets GRADUALLY LOUDER.
   • Add a DIMINUENDO sign ( ) UNDER the staff if the melody gets GRADUALLY SOFTER.

1

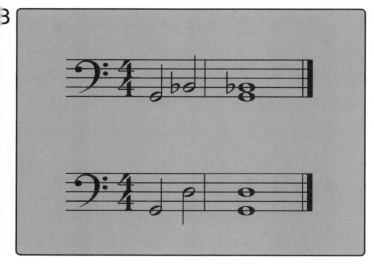

2

3

4

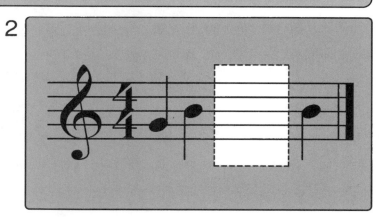

5

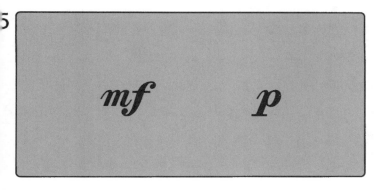

6

TEACHER: See page 43.

Use with page 6.

Intervals

Your teacher will play MELODIC intervals of a 2nd, 3rd, 4th or 5th above the given note.

• Draw the second note on the staff using a half note.

• Write the interval number (2, 3, 4 or 5) on the line.

1

2

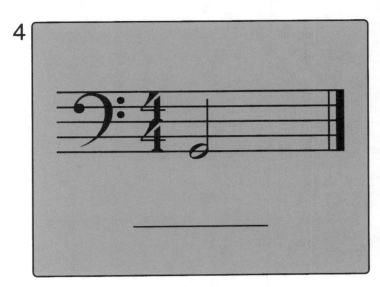

3

4

5

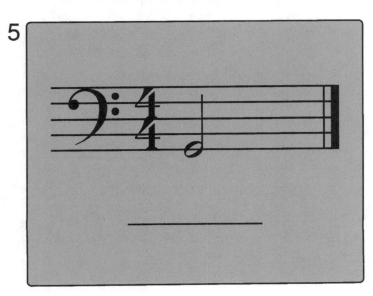

6

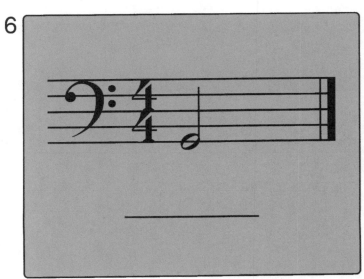

TEACHER: See page 43.

G Position

Your teacher will play melodies in the G POSITION.

Draw the missing two eighth notes () in the box.

Use with page 8.

Positions

- Color the keys on the keyboard RED for the right hand G POSITION.
- Color the keys on the keyboard BLUE for the left hand G POSITION.
- Color the keys on the keyboard YELLOW for the left hand an octave higher G POSITION.
- Color the keys on the keyboard GREEN for the right hand C POSITION.
- Color the keys on the keyboard PURPLE for the left hand C POSITION.

1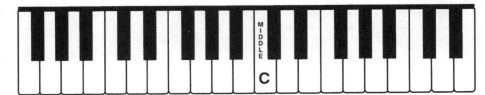

2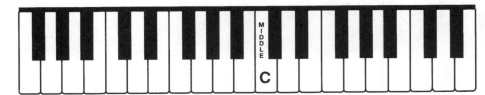

3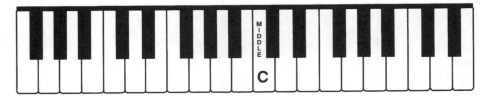

4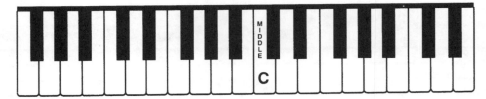

5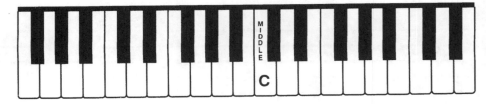

Rhythm Patterns

Your teacher will clap a rhythm pattern.

Circle the pattern that you hear.

1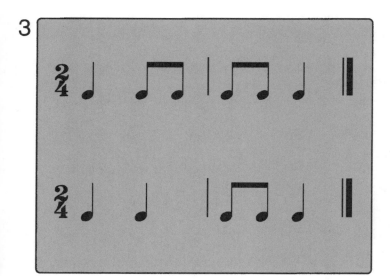

2

3

4

5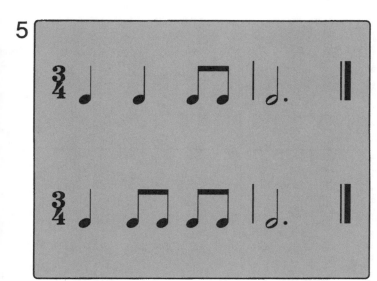

6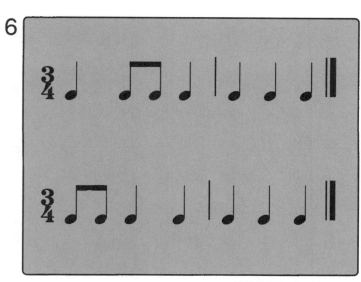

Use with pages 10–11.

Intervals

Your teacher will play groups of HARMONIC intervals.

Circle the group of intervals that you hear.

1

2

3
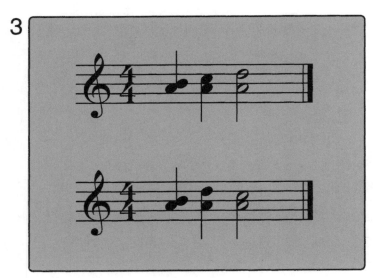

4
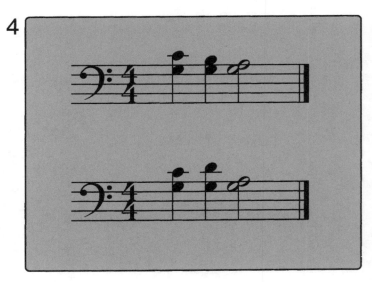

5
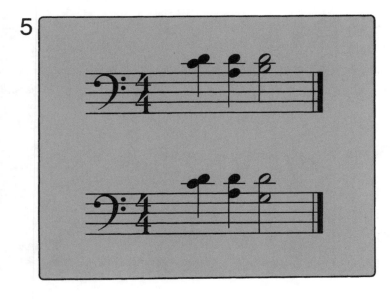

6
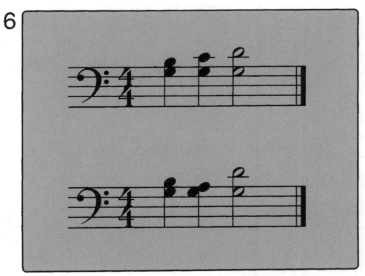

TEACHER: See page 43.

G POSITION

Your teacher will play melodies in the G POSITION.

One note in each melody will be played incorrectly. Circle the incorrect note.

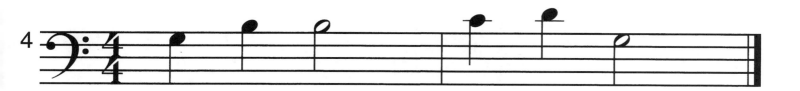

Use with page 13.

One Octave Higher or Lower

Your teacher will play each melody two times. The second time it will be played one octave higher or one octave lower.

- Circle HIGHER if the melody is played ONE OCTAVE HIGHER.
- Circle LOWER if the melody is played ONE OCTAVE LOWER.

1

HIGHER

LOWER

2

HIGHER

LOWER

3

HIGHER

LOWER

4

HIGHER

LOWER

5

HIGHER

LOWER

6

HIGHER

LOWER

TEACHER: See page 44.

Rhythm Patterns

Your teacher will clap a rhythm pattern.

Draw the missing notes in the second measure, using  or ♩♩♩♩

1.

2.

3.

4.

5.

6.

TEACHER: See page 44.

Use with pages 16–17.

Tempo Marks

Your teacher will play ALLEGRO and MODERATO melodies.
- Circle ALLEGRO if the melody is played QUICKLY, HAPPILY.
- Circle MODERATO if the melody is played MODERATELY.

1

_____ *Allegro*

Moderato

2

_____ *Allegro*

Moderato

3

_____ *Allegro*

Moderato

4

_____ *Allegro*

Moderato

5

_____ *Allegro*

Moderato

6

_____ *Allegro*

Moderato

TEACHER: See page 44.

Intervals

- Color the keys on the keyboard RED for the MELODIC INTERVALS.
- Color the keys on the keyboard BLUE for the HARMONIC INTERVALS.
- Write the interval name (2, 3, 4 or 5) on the line.

1 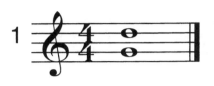 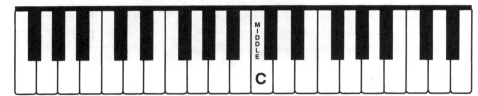 ___

2 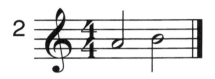 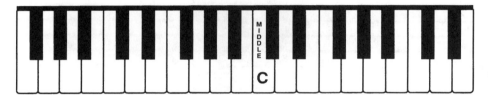 ___

3   ___

4 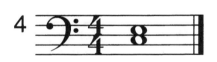 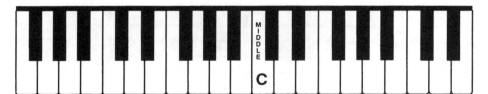 ___

5  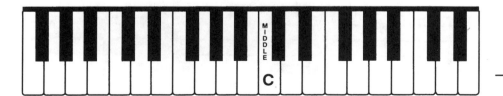 ___

6  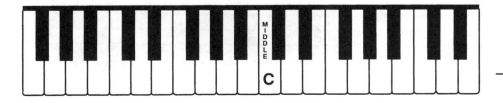 ___

Use with page 18.

Four Positions

Your teacher will play melodies in the C, D, E and F positions.

Draw the missing quarter note (♩) or two eighth notes (♫) in the box.

TEACHER: See page 44.

Positions

- Color the keys on the keyboard RED for the C POSITION.
- Color the keys on the keyboard BLUE for the D POSITION
- Color the keys on the keyboard YELLOW for E POSITION.
- Color the keys on the keyboard GREEN for the F POSITION.
- Color the keys on the keyboard PURPLE for the G POSITION.

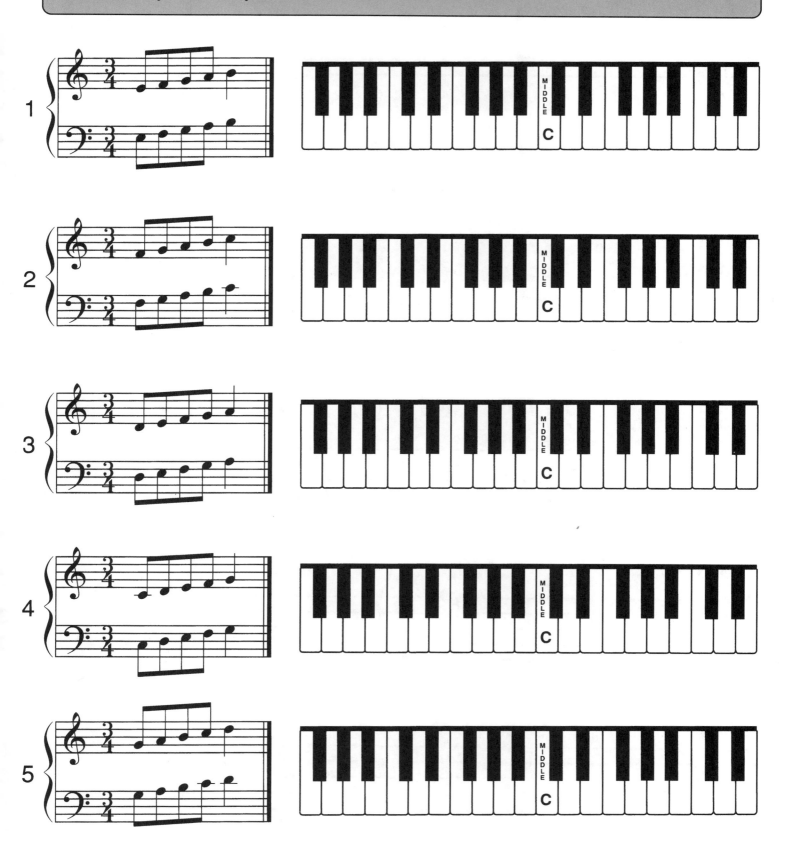

Use with pages 20–21.

Flat

Your teacher will play each melody two times. The second time that it is played a flat will be added to one note. Draw a flat (♭) in front of the appropriate note.

Rhythm Patterns

Your teacher will clap a rhythm pattern.

Write the pattern that you hear.

1
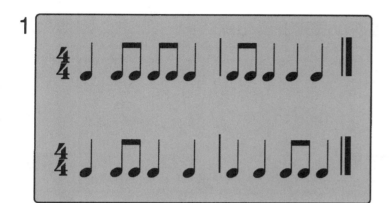

Pattern: _____

2
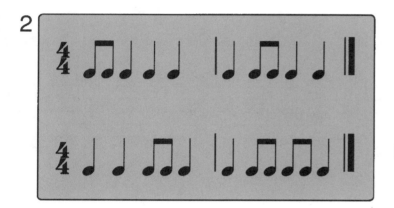

Pattern: _____

3
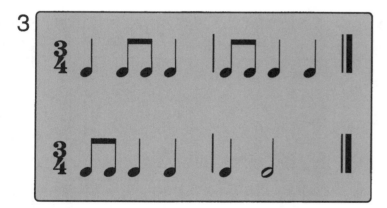

Pattern: _____

4
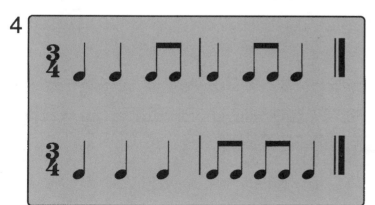

Pattern: _____

Use with page 22.

The Damper Pedal

Your teacher will play six melodies.

Draw a PEDAL SIGN (⌐_____⌐) under the entire melody if the DAMPER PEDAL is used.

TEACHER: See page 45.

Positions

- Color the keys on the keyboard RED for the notes from the C POSITION.
- Color the keys on the keyboard BLUE for the notes from the D POSITION
- Color the keys on the keyboard YELLOW for the notes from the E POSITION.
- Color the keys on the keyboard GREEN for the notes from the F POSITION.
- Color the keys on the keyboard PURPLE for the notes from the G POSITION.

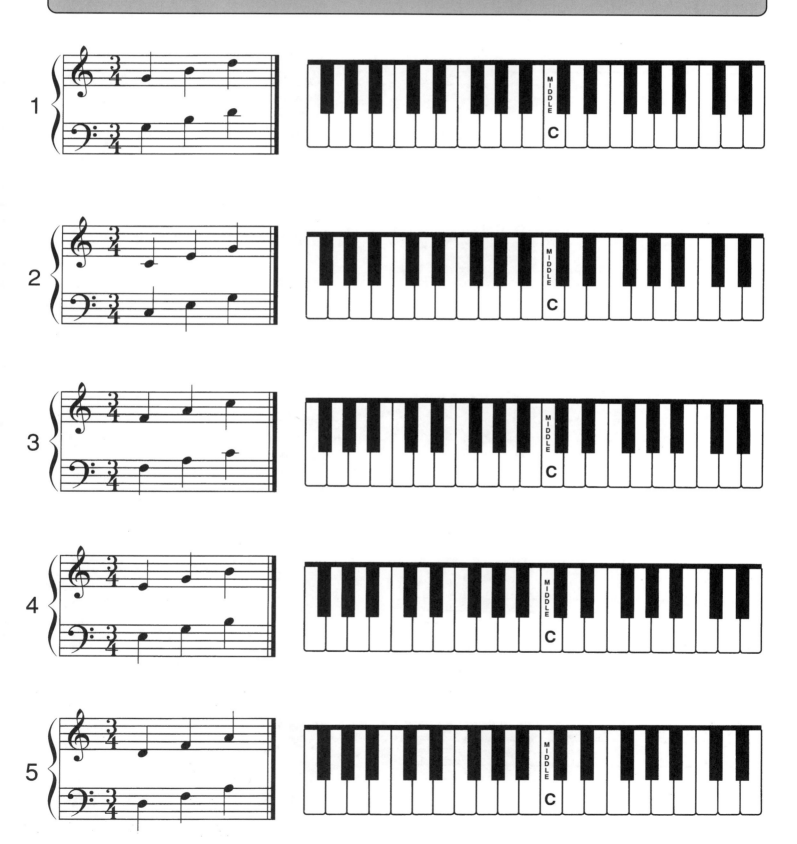

Use with pages 24–25.

One Octave Higher or Lower

Your teacher will play each pattern two times. The second time it will be played one octave higher or one octave lower.

- Circle HIGHER if the melody is played ONE OCTAVE HIGHER.
- Circle LOWER if the melody is played ONE OCTAVE LOWER.

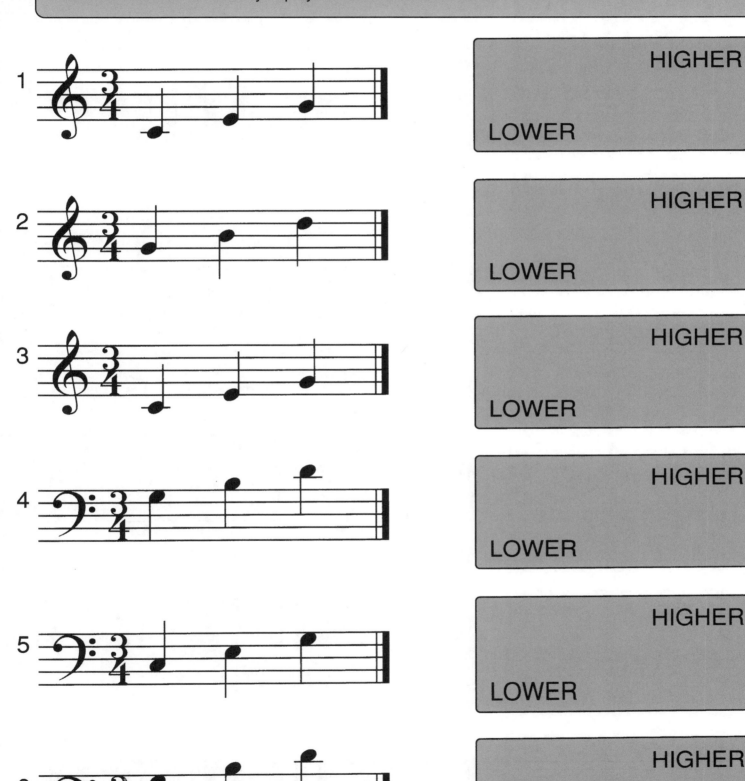

1   HIGHER   LOWER

2   HIGHER   LOWER

3   HIGHER   LOWER

4   HIGHER   LOWER

5   HIGHER   LOWER

6   HIGHER   LOWER

TEACHER: See page 45.

2nds and 3rds

Your teacher will play HARMONIC intervals or MELODIC patterns using 2nds and 3rds.

Circle the interval or pattern that you hear.

1

2

3

4
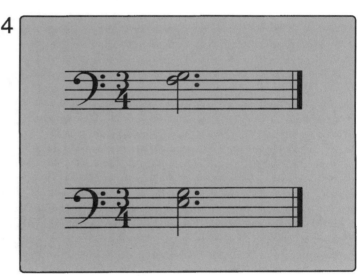

5
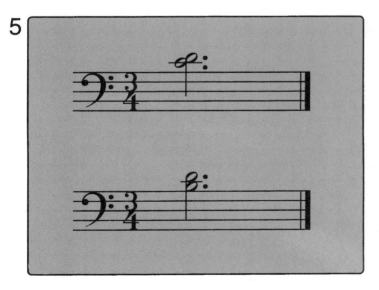

6
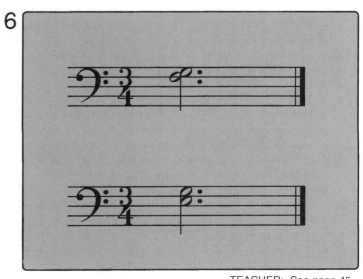

TEACHER: See page 45.

Use with page 26.

Half Steps

Your teacher will play a HALF STEP that moves UP or DOWN.

- If the second note moves UP a HALF STEP, draw a SHARP (♯) in front of it.
- If the second note moves DOWN a HALF STEP, draw a FLAT (♭) in front of it.

1

2

3

4

5

6
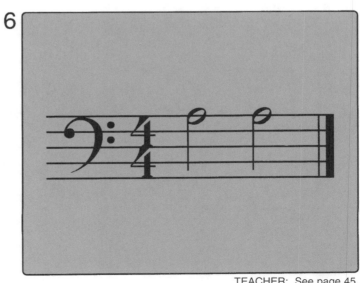

TEACHER: See page 45.

Half Steps

Your teacher will play melodies containing HALF STEPS.

Circle the melody that you hear.

1

2

3

4

5

6

TEACHER: See page 45.

Use with pages 28–29.

Rhythm Patterns

Your teacher will clap a rhythm pattern.

Circle the pattern that you hear.

1

2

3

4
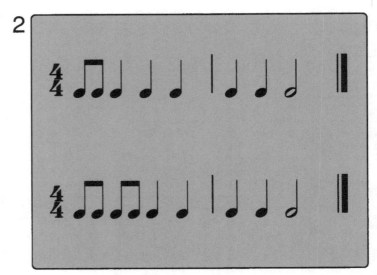

5
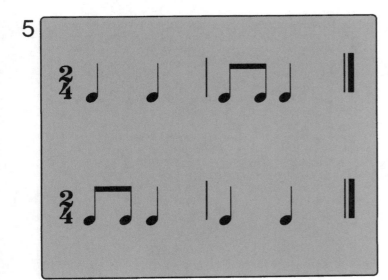

6
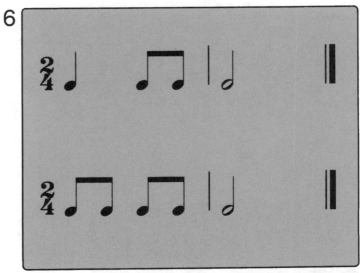

Whole Steps

Your teacher will play a WHOLE STEP that moves UP or DOWN.

Draw the second note on the staff using a half note.

1

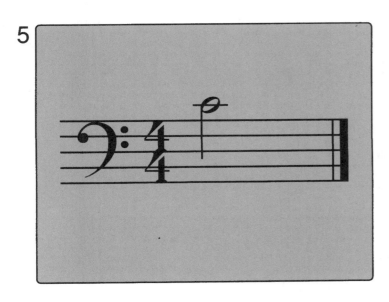

2

3

4

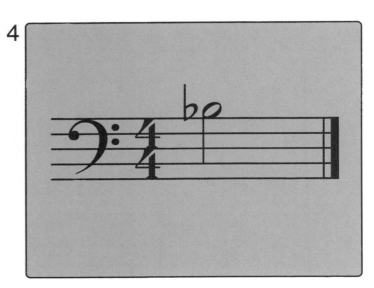

5

6

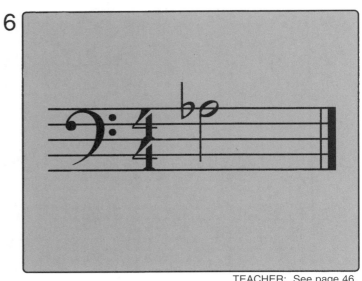

TEACHER: See page 46.

Use with page 31.

Whole Steps

Your teacher will play melodies containing WHOLE STEPS.

Circle the melody that you hear.

1

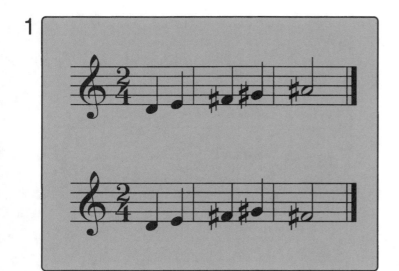

2

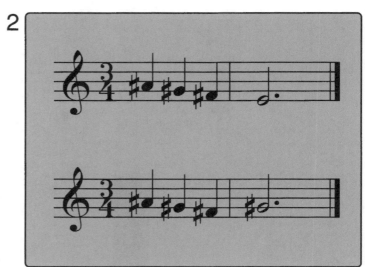

3

4

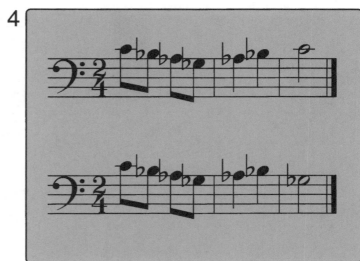

5

6

TEACHER: See page 46.

Half and Whole Steps

Your teacher will play a HALF STEP or a WHOLE STEP.

Circle the example that you hear.

1

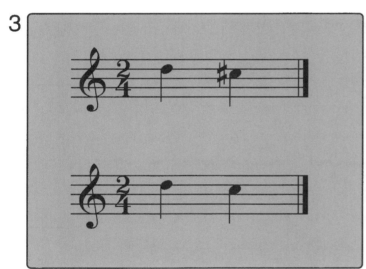

2

3

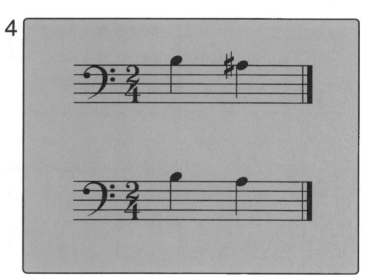

4

5

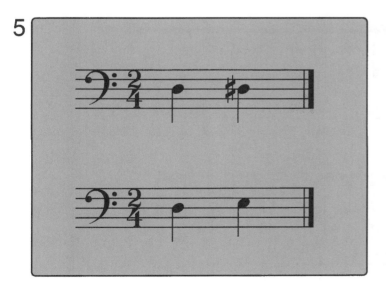

6

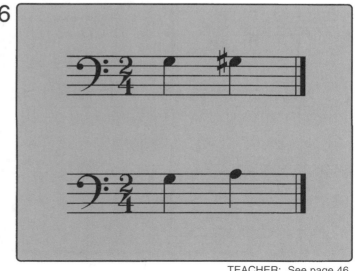

TEACHER: See page 46.

Use with pages 32–33.

Half and Whole Steps

- Color the appropriate keys RED for the HALF STEPS.
- Color the appropriate keys BLUE for the WHOLE STEPS.
- Write H for HALF STEP or W for WHOLE STEP on the line.

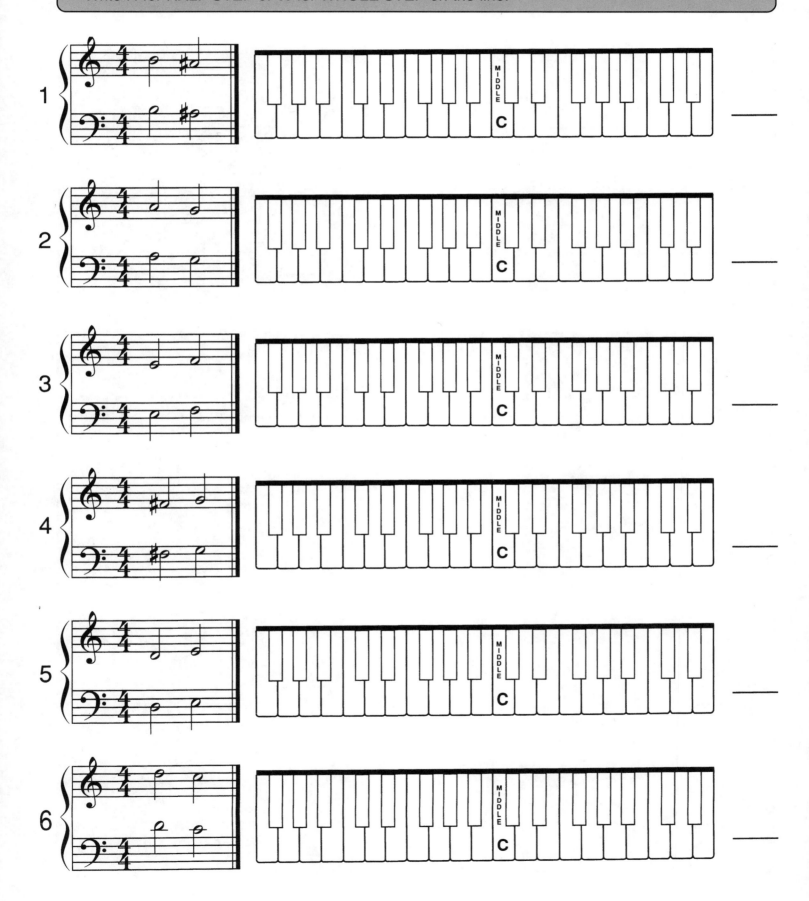

Staccato

Your teacher will play six melodies.

Add a STACCATO DOT under ( ) or over ( ) each note that is played staccato.

TEACHER: See page 46.

Crescendo and Diminuendo

Your teacher will play six melodies.

- Add a CRESCENDO sign (<) UNDER the staff if the melody gets GRADUALLY LOUDER.
- Add a DIMINUENDO sign (>) UNDER the staff if the melody gets GRADUALLY SOFTER.

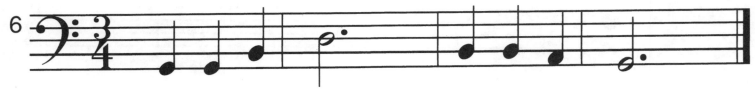

Tetrachords

Your teacher will play four–note TETRACHORD patterns.

Draw the missing note in the box.

1

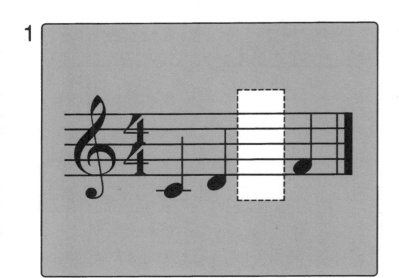

2

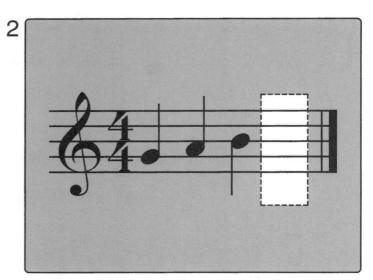

3

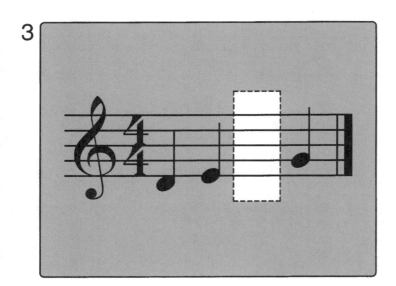

4

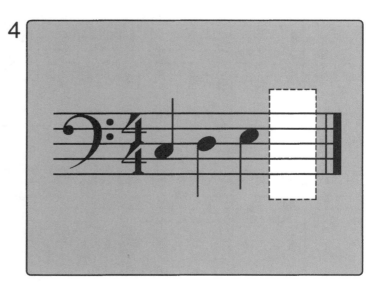

5

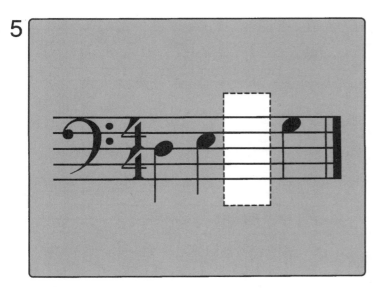

6

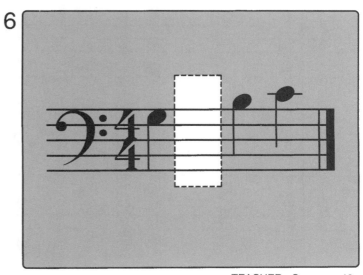

Use with page 37.

The Major Scale

Your teacher will play MAJOR SCALES. One note in each scale will be played incorrectly.

Circle the incorrect note.

Rhythm Patterns

Your teacher will play MAJOR SCALES.

Circle the rhythm pattern that you hear for each scale.

1

2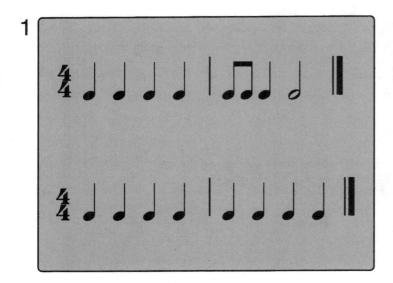

3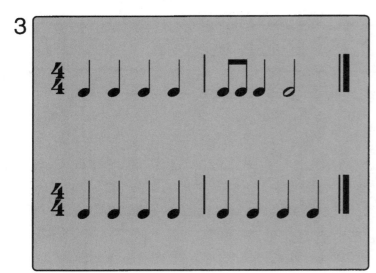

4

5

6

TEACHER: See page 47.

Use with page 39.

Key of G Major

Your teacher will play six melodies in the KEY OF G MAJOR.

Draw the missing note in the box.

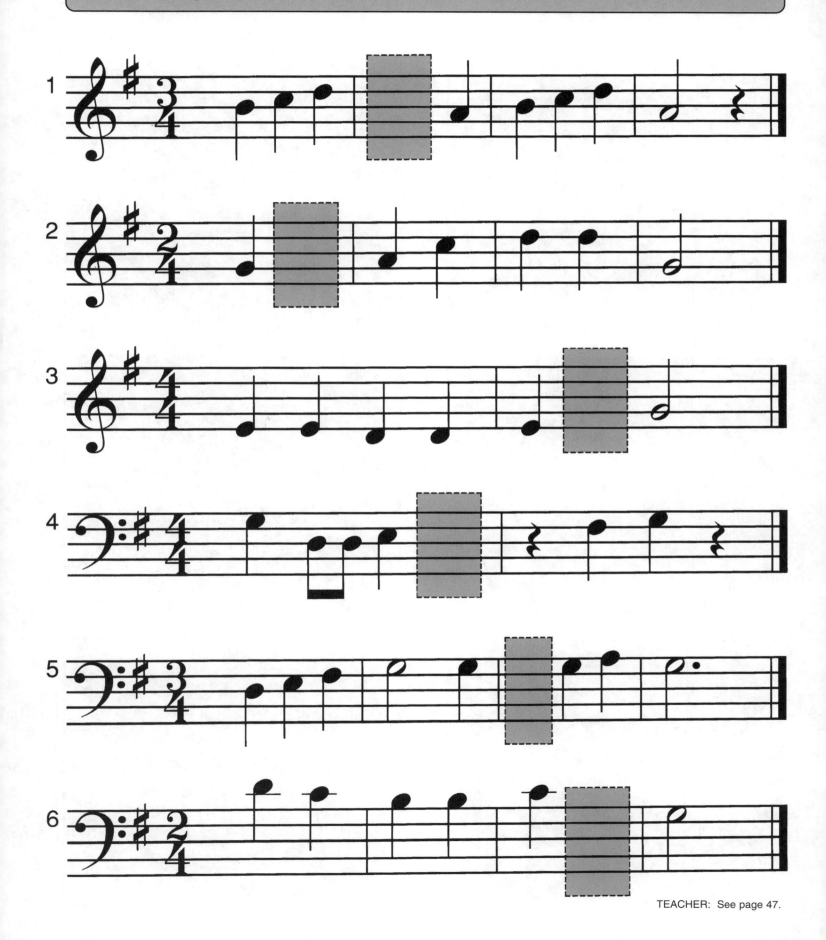

TEACHER: See page 47.

Rhythm Patterns

Your teacher will clap a rhythm pattern.

Draw the missing notes and rests in the third measure, using  and

1.

2.

3.

4.

5.

6.

Use with pages 40–41.

Tempo Marks

Your teacher will play MODERATO and ADAGIO melodies.

- Circle MODERATO if the melody is played MODERATELY.
- Circle ADAGIO if the melody is played SLOWLY.

1

Moderato

Adagio

2

Moderato

Adagio

3

Moderato

Adagio

4

Moderato

Adagio

5

Moderato

Adagio

6

Moderato

Adagio

TEACHER: See page 47.

Sharp

Your teacher will play each melody two times. The second time that it is played a sharp will be added to one note. Draw a sharp (♯) in front of the appropriate note.

TEACHER: See page 48.

Use with pages 44–45.

Intervals

Your teacher will play MELODIC intervals of a 2nd, 3rd, 4th or 5th above the given note.

- Draw the second note on the staff using a half note.
- Write the interval number (2, 3, 4 or 5) on the line.

1

2
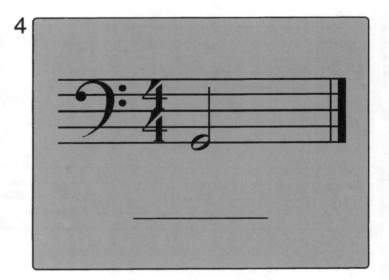

3

4

5

6
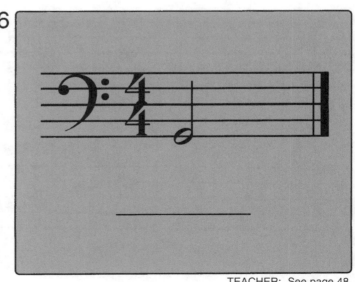

C and G Positions

Your teacher will play melodies in the C and G POSITIONS.

One note in each melody will be played incorrectly. Circle the incorrect note.

Use with page 46.

Time Signatures

Your teacher will play melodies in $\frac{2}{4}$ or $\frac{3}{4}$ time.

- Circle the $\frac{2}{4}$ if you hear 2 beats in each measure.

- Circle the $\frac{3}{4}$ if you hear 3 beats in each measure.

1

$\frac{2}{4}$ $\frac{3}{4}$

2

$\frac{2}{4}$ $\frac{3}{4}$

3

$\frac{2}{4}$ $\frac{3}{4}$

4

$\frac{2}{4}$ $\frac{3}{4}$

5

$\frac{2}{4}$ $\frac{3}{4}$

6

$\frac{2}{4}$ $\frac{3}{4}$

TEACHER: See page 48.

Review

1. Your teacher will play a MELODIC interval of a 2nd, 3rd, 4th or 5th above the given note.
   - Draw the second note on the staff using a half note.
   - Write the interval number (2, 3, 4 or 5) on the line.
2. Your teacher will clap a rhythm pattern. Circle the pattern that you hear.
3. Your teacher will play a group of HARMONIC intervals. Circle the group of intercals that you hear.
4. Your teacher will play a melody two times. The second time that it is played a flat will be added to one note. Draw a flat (♭) in front of the appropriate note.
5. Your teacher will play a pattern two times. The second time it will be played one octave higher or one octave lower.
   - Circle HIGHER if the melody is played ONE OCTAVE HIGHER.
   - Circle LOWER if the melody is played ONE OCTAVE LOWER.
6. Your teacher will play a MAJOR SCALE. One note will be played incorrectly. Circle the incorrect note.

2

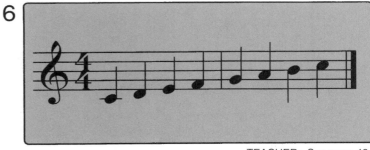

4

5

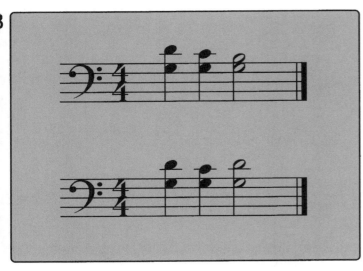

6

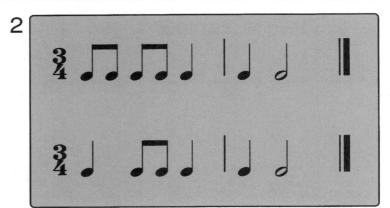

TEACHER: See page 48.

Use with page 47.

Review

1. Your teacher will clap a rhythm pattern.
   Draw the missing notes in the second measure using ♩ ♫♩ or ♫♫♩

2. Your teacher will play a melody in the G POSITION. Draw the missing quarter note (♩) or two eighth notes (♫) in the box.

3. Your teacher will play an ALLEGRO or MODERATO melody.
   • Circle ALLEGRO if the melody is played QUICKLY, HAPPILY.
   • Circle MODERATO if the melody is played MODERATELY.

4. Your teacher will play a melody. Draw a PEDAL SIGN (└─────┘) under the entire melody if the DAMPER PEDAL is used.

5. Your teacher will play a HALF STEP that moves UP or DOWN.
   • If the note moves UP a HALF STEP, draw a SHARP (♯) in front of it.
   • If the note moves DOWN a HALF STEP, draw a FLAT (♭) in front of it.

6. Your teacher will play a WHOLE STEP that moves UP or DOWN.
   Draw the second note on the staff using a half note.

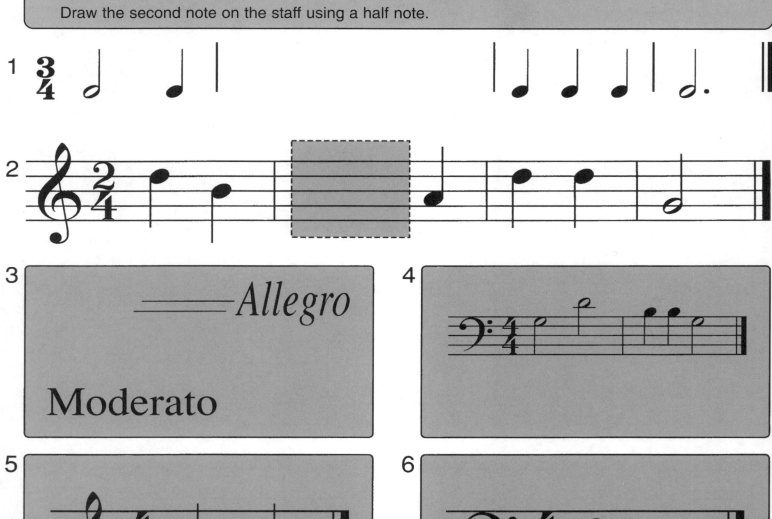

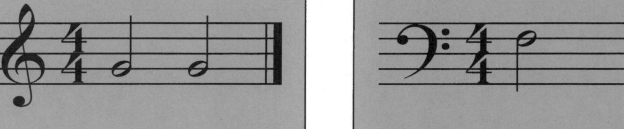

TEACHER: See page 48.

43

Teacher's Examples

Page 3 (Clap)

Page 4 (Play)

Page 5 (Play)

Page 7 (Clap)

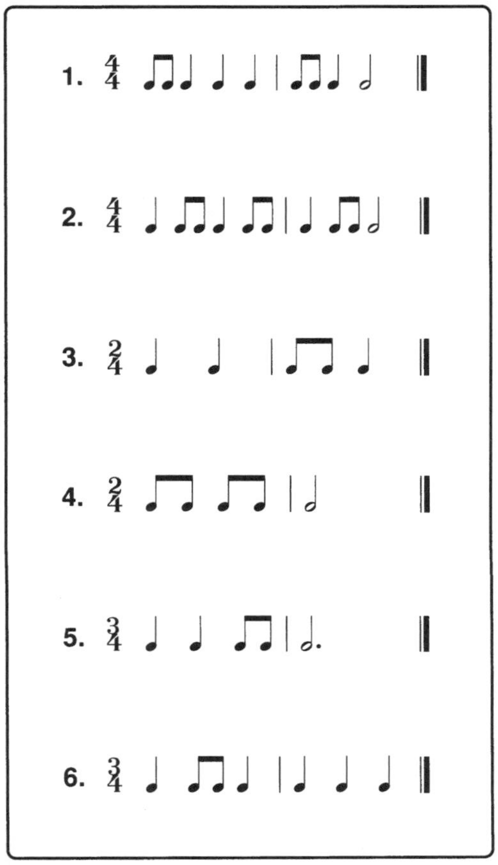

Page 8 (Play)

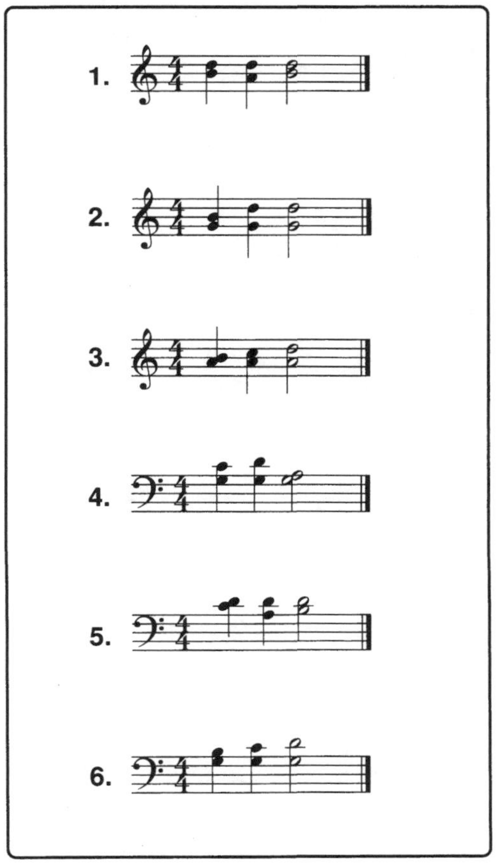

Page 9 (Play)

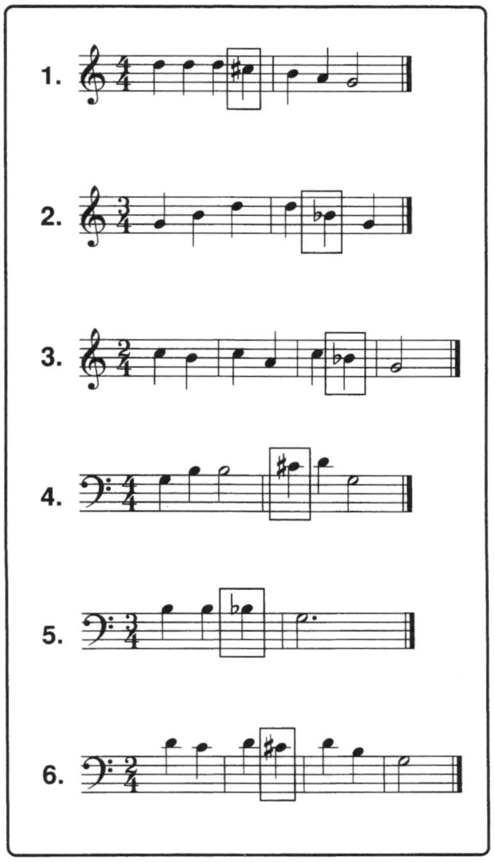

Teacher's Examples

Page 10 (Play)

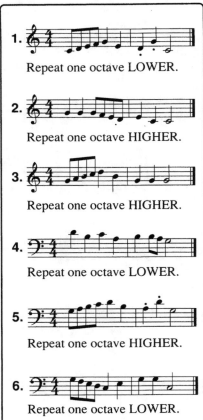

1. Repeat one octave LOWER.

2. Repeat one octave HIGHER.

3. Repeat one octave HIGHER.

4. Repeat one octave LOWER.

5. Repeat one octave HIGHER.

6. Repeat one octave LOWER.

Page 11 (Clap)

Page 12 (Play)

Page 14 (Play)

Page 16 (Play)

Play each example twice. The first time the flatted note [(♭)♩] should be played as a natural; the second time it should be played as a flat.

Page 17 (Clap)

Teacher's Examples

Page 18 (Play)

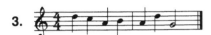

Page 20 (Play)

Repeat one octave HIGHER.

Repeat one octave HIGHER.

Repeat one octave LOWER.

Repeat one octave LOWER.

Repeat one octave LOWER.

Repeat one octave HIGHER.

Page 21 (Play)

Page 22 (Play)

Page 23 (Play)

Page 24 (Clap)

Teacher's Examples

Page 25 (Play)

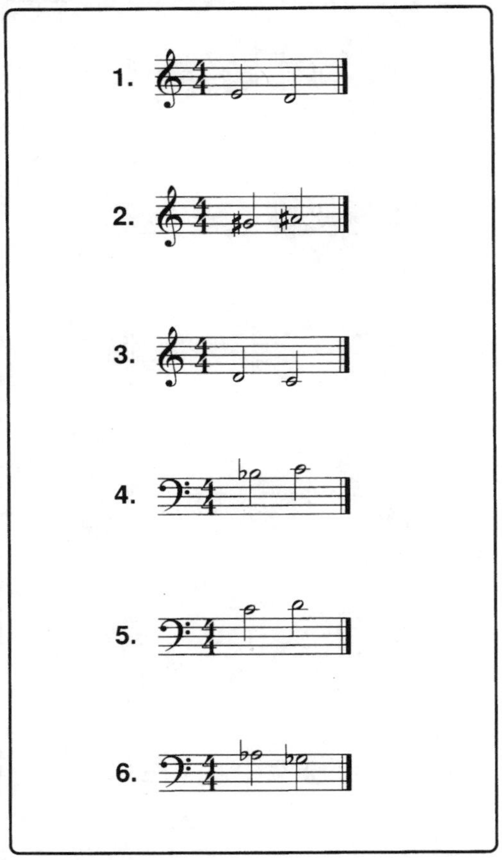

Page 26 (Play)

Page 27 (Play)

Page 29 (Play)

Page 30 (Play)

Page 31 (Play)

47

Teacher's Examples

Page 32 (Play)

Page 33 (Play)

Page 34 (Play)

Page 35 (Clap)

Page 36 (Play)

48

Teacher's Examples

Page 37 (Play)

Play each example twice. The first time the sharped note [(♯)♩] should be played as a natural; the second time it should be played as a sharp.

1.

2.

3.

4.

5.

6.

Page 38 (Play)

1.   **2**

2.   **5**

3.   **3**

4.   **4**

5.   **5**

6.   **3**

Page 39 (Play)

1.

2.

3.

4.

5.

6.

Page 40 (Play)

1.

2.

3.

4.

5.

6.

Page 41 (Play)

1.   **5**

(Clap)

2.

(Play)

3.

4.

5.

Repeat one octave HIGHER.

6.

Page 42 (Clap)

1.

(Play)

2.

Allegro

3.

4.

5.

6.